Surviving Your Season of Shame

Surviving Your Season of Shame

Overcoming Life's Most Embarrassing Moments

Catrina M. Blount

Surviving Your Season of Shame
Copyright © 2015 by Catrina M. Blount. All rights reserved.

No part of this publication may be reproduced, stored in a retrieval system or transmitted in any way by any means, electronic, mechanical, photocopy, recording or otherwise without the prior permission of the author except as provided by USA copyright law.

Scripture quotations marked (KJV) are taken from the *Holy Bible, King James Version*, Cambridge, 1769. Used by permission. All rights reserved.

Unless otherwise noted, scripture quotations are taken from the *Holy Bible, New International Version®*, NIV® Copyright ©1984 by Biblica, Inc.® Used by permission. All rights reserved worldwide.

Scripture quotations marked (HCSB) are taken from the *Holman Christian Standard Bible*. Copyright 2004 Holman Bible Publishers.

This book is designed to provide accurate information with regard to the subject matter covered; however, it is written from the perspective of the author's own personal experiences. This information is given with the understanding that the author is not engaged in rendering legal, professional advice, nor is the author providing counseling of any kind. Since the details of your situation are fact dependent, you should seek the services of a competent professional if needed. Some names and identifying details have been changed to protect the privacy of individuals.

Cover design by Samson Lim
Interior design by Manolito Bastasa

Published in the United States of America

ISBN: 978-0-69296-982-3
1. Religion / Christian Life / Personal Growth
2. Religion / Christian Life / Inspirational
15.10.07

ACKNOWLEDGMENTS

Praises be to God, who always causes us to triumph!

All of the events taken from my life are commonly known by those who know me best. For some of you, this will explain a lot about the way I act. To be honest, I was worried about some of the things that I felt God leading me to tell. But I have tested them out on some extraordinary people who I know would tell me if I had gone too far. As part of my acknowledgments, I would like to say a special thank you to them for being what I call my screening committee: Pastor J. Melinda Clay, Rev. Anna Kennedy, and Minister Chris Lee.

I give honor to my mother, Polley Page, for all of the effort she put into raising me and for her consistent support of everything I try—cosmetics sales, writing, modeling, singing, preaching, and teaching. Mom, at all times and in all things, you are my rock.

I thank my husband, Darryl, for agreeing with me that our story was meaningful to this book. I bless him for allowing me to expose our drama to help someone survive.

To the rest of my family—Erris, Shondia, Tonja, Mary, Rose, Anthony, Xavier, Brielle, and Lauryn—I love you with all that I am. Thank you for being there for me.

And thank you, Eleanor and Charmaine, for your keen eyes, editorial work, honest feedback, and enthusiasm for this project.

Finally, thank you to the wonderful staff at Tate Publishing and Enterprises LLC for taking my diamond in the rough and polishing it until it far outshined anything I could imagine.

God bless and rain peace upon you all.

Contents

Introduction 9

1 It's Only for a Season 17
2 There's Purpose in the Season 27
3 You're Anointed in Each Season 41
4 Praise God in the Season 63
5 God Restores in Due Season 83
6 Final Thoughts 97

INTRODUCTION

EVERY SO OFTEN, something happens that can be genuinely seen as inspirational-above and beyond the ordinary events of life. One night in May 2007, as I was studying and praying, the following event took place. I wrote it down just like this that night, and I have tried to remain faithful to the revelation just as it was given to me. This event is the catalyst behind everything else you read in this book.

The Spirit of the Lord said, "Read," and so I read the words of the book of Isaiah, stopping by the unction of the Spirit. And when He said, "Write," indeed, I did write a summation of the things I read. And when I asked the meaning, this is what I heard:

> It is time, saith the Lord, for those that I have anointed to come out of obscurity. Many have advanced in My name without the benefit of My

anointing. Yet a little while, and I will pull their cover off and expose their heart. Many will fall away because of those whose hearts are not with Me. In that day I will bring up out of shame My anointed. They shall set in order the things that remain, and I will reward them double for their shame. I will empower my righteous ones to rebuild the waste places of America and to bind the open wounds. Peace shall be found in them, and I will appoint servants to watch over their goods. Surely my righteous ones shall prosper and be known as those that do love and serve Me. I am preparing My righteous ones in their season of shame. Surely I will teach them to endure. Surely I will spread My wings over them, although I will remove to a distance. In their season of shame they will hear My voice clearly and rejoice. They shall know that I require righteousness. They shall call, and I will answer, even in their season of shame. A new tongue and a new praise will I prepare for them. At My set time, I will pull down, and at My set time, I will restore. I will not hide My set hour from My righteous ones, for they shall hear and speak of that time, saith the Lord. And I will set on high those that have proven themselves in their season of shame.

The Scripture I read was Isaiah 61:1–9, KJV:

> The Spirit of the Lord GOD [is] upon me; because the LORD hath anointed me to preach good tidings unto the meek; he hath sent me to bind up the brokenhearted, to proclaim liberty to the captives, and the opening of the prison to [them that are] bound; To proclaim the acceptable year of the LORD, and the day of vengeance of our God; to comfort all that mourn; To appoint unto them that mourn in Zion, to give unto them beauty for ashes, the oil of joy for mourning, the garment of praise for the spirit of heaviness; that they might be called trees of righteousness, the planting of the LORD, that he might be glorified. And they shall build the old wastes, they shall raise up the former desolations, and they shall repair the waste cities, the desolations of many generations. And strangers shall stand and feed your flocks, and the sons of the alien [shall be] your plowmen and your vinedressers. But ye shall be named the Priests of the LORD: [men] shall call you the Ministers of our God: ye shall eat the riches of the Gentiles, and in their glory shall ye boast yourselves. For your shame [ye shall have] double; and [for] confusion they shall rejoice in their por-

tion: therefore in their land they shall possess the double: everlasting joy shall be unto them. For I the LORD love judgment, I hate robbery for burnt offering; and I will direct their work in truth, and I will make an everlasting covenant with them. And their seed shall be known among the Gentiles, and their offspring among the people: all that see them shall acknowledge them, that they [are] the seed [which] the LORD hath blessed.

The Holy Ghost gave me the following points to ponder from that passage:

(1) We must first acknowledge our anointing and its purpose.
(2) There must be a rebuilding of ruins and devastations.
(3) Others will be put to work on our behalf tending what is ours.
(4) Others will call us priests and lift us up as God's ministers.
(5) We will receive wealth and riches from foreign sources.
(6) We will have a double portion to replace our shame.
(7) A joyous shout will replace our humiliation.
(8) We will keep a double portion in our own land.
(9) The Lord hates unrighteous ministry.

(10) The Lord will direct those that are in covenant with Him.

Not long before this, Pastor Shelia Pittman of The Rock Ministries International in Humble, Texas, preached a message that had already begun changing the way I felt about the many seasons of shame in my life. The title was "Private Preparation by Public Humiliation." Through that message, I was encouraged yet again to understand that God works everything according to the counsel of His own will, and He causes all things to work together for our good (Rom. 8:28).

I kept coming back to that prophetic word, amazed that the Spirit of God would share such a revelation with me. What was I supposed to do with it? Who was I supposed to release it to? Once I understood that shame had a purpose, how could I encourage someone else with the news? And when I heard the message from Pastor Pittman, I wondered over and over what God was preparing me for during the various seasons of shame in my life. What was the purpose for my shame?

It was these questions that gave birth to this book. I always told my Sunday school and ministry students that when God lets you see a problem and no one else seems to see it, it's because He has given you a solution. You are the one who is supposed to do something about it. With that in mind, I sat down to write about living past the lingering shadow of shame. Unfortunately, life intervened and gave me new material for the book. Not only that, I realized as I wrote that I really hadn't healed from some of the experiences I was writing about. Because the feelings came to the surface in ways that seemed unhealthy to me, I put the book aside and took up other projects. For years, it seemed this was a project that would never be completed.

But I was jolted back into this book through the prompting of the Holy Spirit as I started pondering the suicides of three young men that I was acquainted with in various ways. I did not know what exactly prompted their actions, but it troubled me. What had happened that was so devastating that they could not face life anymore? Was there no one who could have told them that they could make it through their season of shame? These deaths were totally unexpected by these young men's family and friends. They were always there for others, always helping out friends in need. We all wondered what burdens they were carrying that they did not feel safe releasing to anyone, even their pastors and spiritual leaders. I realized that there are many Christians who need to be encouraged that flaws are not final and do not have to be fatal. So after processing, through prayer, every area where I have held on to the sting of shame, I began writing again. The book that you hold in your hands now is meant to encourage you to keep holding on, trusting the Lord to bring you out, no matter what.

It bothers me that in modern Christianity, we are often given a message that would lead us to believe that if we have problems, we are out of the will of God. We have been painted a picture of an always sunny sky, but the Bible teaches us that nearly everyone God used greatly had experience with a season of shame. Lord knows I have had my seasons of shame, and I wrote this book partially in an attempt to come to grips with all that I have been through.

As you read the chapters that follow, it is my prayer that you receive something that will help you hold on until your season of shame is over. Not only that, I hope you will find, as I did, that the season of shame will make you stronger than you can imagine. God uses those seasons to prune us, perfect us, and replant us so that we can bring about a greater return for the Kingdom of God.

1

It's Only for a Season

There is a time for everything, and a season for every activity under heaven: a time to be born and a time to die, a time to plant and a time to uproot, a time to kill and a time to heal, a time to tear down and a time to build, a time to weep and a time to laugh, a time to mourn and a time to dance, a time to scatter stones and a time to gather them, a time to embrace and a time to refrain, a time to search and a time to give up, a time to keep and a time to throw away, a time to tear and a time to mend, a time to be silent and a time to speak, a time to love and a time to hate, a time for war and a time for peace.

—Ecclesiastes 3:1–8

When I was in eighth grade, I got pregnant. Now in those days, the early eighties, that was not as common as it is now. There was reaction from every quarter—my mom's profound disappointment, my peers shying away from the "fast girl," and teachers and school administrators treating me with disdain.

One particular incident stays forever etched in my memory. One morning at Fondren Middle School, the assistant principal (I won't name her, although I can never forget her name) walked up to me right before the first bell was to ring. She said, "I understand that you are pregnant. Whatcha gonna name the baby?" Thinking that for once someone was really interested in me, I told her I didn't know yet and that I didn't know whether it was a boy or a girl. With a sneer on her face, that woman—that adult—said to me, a thirteen-year-old child, "You need to name the baby Skippy, because that's all you've done since you've been here."

With tears in my eyes and half the student body laughing at me, my season of shame was in full effect. I thought it would never end. When I walked the halls, I would hear whispers and "Skippy" being snarled everywhere around me. The kids that I had known for all of my middle school years were suddenly making me the butt of the funniest joke ever. It was almost more than I could take. But one thing helped me get through it all: the knowledge that neither middle school nor pregnancy would last forever. I didn't know that at first and tried to think of everything I could to get out of going to school and away from those that tormented me. It was my mom that helped me gain the perspective I needed. She had, ironically, been a teenage parent and was well acquainted with the stigma attached to it.

Before I really knew anything about the Bible, I learned the very valuable lesson taught in Ecclesiastes 3: everything has a season, even embarrassment. God works through times and seasons to accomplish His purposes on the earth. What I learned is that although the Bible says there is a time for everything, everything does not happen at the same time. In looking through the Bible, I find that many of its characters have lessons to teach on surviving shame.

All the Days of My Appointed Time

During the most trying times of my life, I quickly identify with Job. Can you imagine how embarrassed Job must have felt? He went from being the man who had everything to being the man who had nothing—well, almost nothing. When his children, his health, and his wealth were gone, Job was left with his wife and three friends. You would think a rich and prosperous man like Job would have attracted the sympathy of many, but the Bible only mentions his wife and three friends.

His wife's response was typical of many when they encounter their season of shame. She told Job to quit, let go, curse God, and die (Job 2:9, KJV). She questioned the fact that he held on to his faith. Neither of them knew that a conference had been held in Heaven, and Job had been chosen by God to show Satan what a man of God was like.

True enough, Job traveled the road from hope to despair and back again with the help of his friends. Isn't it funny how some people's best efforts to comfort you can make you feel worse?

But if you're a Bible reader—and I hope you are—you can find powerful truths in Job's tale of woe, which, by the way, isn't the whole story. (We'll talk about that later.) Job understood that the season he was going through would not—could not—last forever. He said, "If a man die, shall he live again? All the days of my appointed time will I wait, till my change come" (Job 14:14, KJV).

Job had a firm grasp on something that most of us forget when trouble enters our lives—it is for an appointed time, and after that time, change will come. By his statement, scholars and theologians say Job was looking forward to death as a release from his shame. It sounds gruesome, but death is exactly what we should be looking for to end our season of shame.

Now stay with me; don't drop the book and proclaim, "This woman is nuts! I am *not* going to look for death!"

I'm going somewhere with this. To end a season of shame, there must be death, not physically, but mentally and emotionally. The thoughts and feelings that give birth to your shame must die. Like pride. Or your concern for what others are going to think. Yes, most seasons of shame are ended by death. Our ignorance and obliviousness regarding the ways of God have to die. But once they do, and we're able to see that what's happening to us is not about us, our season of shame can come to a close.

Let's go back to my story. At thirteen, I did not have all this theology and philosophy in my head. But once the secret of my pregnancy was out, and everyone knew what was going on, what was the point of being embarrassed? It was true that I had skipped school a lot—no big deal there. What was said to me may have been mean and hurtful, but once I acknowledged the truth of it and came to grips with my responsibility for it, shame seemed to disappear. I was able to concentrate in school and actually made pretty good grades for the remainder of the year. My beautiful daughter was born right before I entered high school, and middle school was gone from my life forever.

Love Affair

I want to talk to you a little more about how death can end a season of shame. In this example, I do want to discuss literal, physical death, for it is the ultimate end of earthly existence. My mind is immediately drawn to Samson, who was born specifically to bring God's people out of Philistine oppression. His parents were given strict orders by God concerning Samson's upbringing. He was to be dedicated to the Lord from his mother's womb. And he was!

From the biblical accounts, it is easy to see that Samson's parents took their instructions seriously. But once Samson was grown, something went terribly wrong. His parents found out that their boy had a weakness for the wrong kind of woman. And they indulged him in that weakness.

I can't go in to all the details of Samson's life here; you can read it all in Judges 13–15 if you like. I need to get to the part relevant to our journey. All of Samson's recorded love affairs ended badly. But the one I want to look at is the one that has been made famous throughout the ages: Samson and Delilah.

Now Delilah was no ordinary girl—at least not to Samson. He had to have her. And so they began an intimate relationship that landed Samson right within his enemy's reach. The only problem was the Philistines knew that even if they managed to catch him, the supernatural strength God gave Samson would make it impossible to hold him. So the Philistines instead began to work on Delilah. They promised her money if she would only get the information they needed to capture Samson. They eventually succeeded in getting her to try to find out the secret of Samson's strength.

Delilah went to work, using all of her feminine wiles on Samson (remember I said he had a weakness for women?). She asked him where his strength came from. To his credit, Samson resisted giving away the secret of his power for a while. He began to play with his temptress, giving her false answers to her pleas.

But as the Bible says, "Can a man take fire in his bosom and his clothes not be burned?" (Prov. 6:27). When Samson gave his false answers, Delilah put them to the test. She lulled him to sleep and tried every one of them. Then she roused him and told him the enemy had come. Samson awoke and broke out of those traps. This happened at least three times in Judges 16. I can't understand why Samson didn't get the message that this woman meant him no good, but that's another story.

For whatever reason, Samson played the game until the game played him. Delilah nagged and pleaded, even employing the "if you love me" card, which leads a lot of us into embarrassment, until he finally told her the truth—he revealed the secret of his power. And she knew it was the truth. She sent for the Philistines and put them on alert. Then she put Samson to sleep, had his head shaved, and ushered him into his season of shame.

When the Philistines came, Samson rose, thinking he would shake off trouble like he always did. The Bible lets us know that he was unaware that the Lord's presence was no longer with him (Judg. 16:20). What a sad testimony! But it is a testimony many of us share. We step out of God's presence without even being aware of it. But that's a lesson for another day.

Back to Samson's trouble. The Philistines bound Samson, blinded him, and made him a slave in the prison, attaching him to the grinding stone. They rejoiced for many days that their greatest enemy was now in their hands. In fact, they praised their god for allowing them to take Samson down. While they were celebrating, someone decided it would be a good idea to bring Samson out and make fun of him in front of all the people. He had already been humiliated beyond belief, going from conqueror to being conquered. But the Philistines wanted to add insult to injury.

Triumph Over Tormentors

But remember, I told you that shame is only for a season. This is how you know you're at the end of a season of shame: instead of being a mockery, you become mighty! What no one around Samson seemed to notice was that his hair began to grow again (Judg. 16:22). His strength was returning! Samson was brought out, and although he was blind, he remembered the heights from which he had fallen. Samson prayed and asked God to avenge him. Furthermore, God granted his request. He was able to grab hold of the pillars of the stadium the Philistines meant to use to make him a public spectacle. He cried out to God, asking God to let him die with his oppressors, and again, God granted his request.

Samson's season of shame ended with death. But that's not all. Samson killed more Philistines in his death than he ever did in his life (Judg. 16:30). And so will you. In the season of shame, you gain new strength and prepare for a new level of victory. And just when it seems things can't get any worse, you die. The good news is your mental and emotional death turns the tables on those who want to see you swallowed up in shame. You can begin to shout victoriously because death is swallowed up in victory! (1 Cor. 15:54)

Survival Strategies

- ❖ Consider your current situation realistically. How? Avoid the tendency to go to extremes. In other words, don't give in to despair, and don't talk as if your situation does not exist. It is important that you are honest about what you are going through. It is okay to acknowledge that you are not equipped to handle the situation. We have a God who is!

- ❖ Know that God is working behind the scenes, and He doesn't always let you in on His plans. God gives us glimpses—sometimes—of the unseen world, but that does not happen all the time. We have to be confident that whatever we are facing in the natural, there is a corresponding event in the spiritual realm. God may have pointed you out!
- ❖ Know that God puts a limit on what Satan can do to you. We can be even more confident knowing that He is in control and will only allow adverse situations to take us so far before He comes to our aid. Satan does not have all power—God does!
- ❖ Ask God to restore your strength in due time. During your season of shame, you may feel devoid of strength. At times, you feel that you simply cannot go on. These are the times when it is most important to call out to God. Ask Him, by His Holy Spirit, to renew your strength so that you can come out of your trial with victory.

2

There's Purpose in the Season

"Do not be afraid; you will not suffer shame. Do not fear disgrace; you will not be humiliated. You will forget the shame of your youth and remember no more the reproach of your widowhood. For your Maker is your husband—the Lord Almighty is his name—the Holy One of Israel is your Redeemer; he is called the God of all the earth. The Lord will call you back as if you were a wife deserted and distressed in spirit—a wife who married young, only to be rejected," says your God. "For a brief moment I abandoned you, but with deep compassion I will bring you back. In a surge of anger I hid my face from you for a moment, but with everlasting kindness I will have compassion on you," says the Lord your Redeemer.

—Isaiah 54:4–8

Before I got married the first time, I went through a profound season of shame. I became sexually involved with a minister at the church I attended at that time. Even though I knew it was wrong, I loved him, and I believed that he loved me. I was eighteen when I met him, and he was our youth pastor. Within a few years, we went from a friendship that seemed incredibly strong to a more personal relationship that colored every aspect of my life.

Imagine my surprise when the love of my life took a weekend trip without me and came back engaged to another young lady that attended our church! He even announced the engagement to the church over the pulpit. Though it hurt like crazy, there were very few people who really knew I was in a relationship with this man, so I tried to carry on like everything was all right in my life and with me. You know it wasn't! My dream world was falling apart, my hopes and dreams shattered, but I tried my best to cope with everything that was happening. I was a single parent, a working mother, and a young one at that. Pressure felt like it was taking over my life.

One evening at church, my pastor began questioning me about how I was doing. As I talked to him about the struggles I faced, I was very careful to leave out my hurt feelings about the over-the-pulpit, in-my-face (at least to me) engagement announcement. However, as all good pastors do, this one began to probe into the area I was trying to keep hidden. "What's really wrong?" he asked. Before I could stop myself, I blurted out, "I've been having an affair with Dex for over two years."

Needless to say, the pastor was surprised. He admitted he thought there was some relationship but did not know that it had progressed to that level. In the days that followed, he began investigating the situation that I inadvertently brought before him. Since the man involved was a minister of the church, and I was active in the teaching and music ministries, the pastor felt (and he was right) that he needed to address the issue and root out the sin in the camp. He confronted the minister, who promptly denied that he had ever been involved with me. This led to me being accused of lying and trying to destroy that man's happiness, not by him or the pastor, but by the others who somehow found out about the situation. The pastor, however, was relentless. He called the minister in and spoke with him again, this time receiving the truth about the entire situation, including the development of the other relationship.

I was made to confess this to my mother. That was not so bad since I suspect she knew or had suspicions. And by that time, I was an adult in my midtwenties. He was made to confess to his fiancée and her parents. But it didn't stop there. Rumors began to fly around the church, and for some reason, it seemed that I was the only bad person! I kept expecting a scarlet *A*—or maybe an *F* for fornicator—to be pinned on me at any moment.

One Wednesday night, we were at church for Bible study. Nothing was unusual about that. But what happened at the beginning of that study marked me for a long time. The pastor stood up and made an announcement. I can't remember the exact words, but it went something like this: "It has come to my attention that members of our congregation and our leadership have been living in sin. One of them [meaning me] willingly confessed, and the other [meaning him] did not. Tonight, I am allowing them an opportunity to repent to the congregation. And for the next two years, Dex will be on suspension and will not be teaching or ministering. Catrina will be on probation, acting in a limited capacity for the period of two years."

He and I were called up to speak to the entire congregation. It was one of the most humiliating moments of my life. After that service, Dex was infuriated with me and refused to speak to me. I was hurt and angry not only because of his reaction, but because people automatically began to shut me out as if they had never done anything wrong. I withdrew from my church activities and stopped answering my phone. My mind kept telling me to leave the church, but my stubborn streak wouldn't let me (I had been going there longer than the other parties involved in the scandal and had been active and faithful until that time). I was determined to recover in the place of my shame.

However, that was not to be. Both Dex and I had a change of heart (at least toward each other). Eventually, he proposed to me, and we got married. Stupid me! Some parts of our marriage were great. We traveled and had fun together. And financially, I was secure and wanted for nothing. Both of our ministries seemed to be developing, and our families got along well. However, the way our relationship started colored every part of it. We tried to overcome it, but it just seemed to always be in the way. He never let me forget that I had ruined him in front of the church.

We actually changed churches and went through a whole lot of drama before our eventual divorce. This season of shame taught me to tell the truth at the first opportunity. If I had been smarter, the initial shame would have prevented one of the gravest mistakes of my life (or so it seemed): my brief but troubled marriage. On the other hand, if I had avoided the marriage, much of the material for this book would have had to be developed in some other, possibly more terrible, way.

Be very sure that every season of shame has a purpose. No matter the origin, whether by our own acts or those of others around us, the outcome is a valuable lesson. And because my earlier seasons had strengthened me, I was able to survive this one knowing that I would make it through with the help of the Lord.

The Bible gives us examples of many people who were put to shame for a purpose. I want to talk about a few of them so that you can see that God has a reason for every season.

A Pregnant Virgin?

When I think of shame being for a purpose, I am reminded of Mary. She was informed by an angel that she had been chosen to mother God's child. Obviously innocent, she asked how she was to become pregnant since she had never been intimate with a man. The angel explained that she would be overshadowed by the Holy Ghost. Mary responded with a statement that has recently become part of my daily prayer: "Be it unto me even as you have said" (Luke 1:38).

But wait a minute; scholars say that Mary was only about thirteen to seventeen years old at the time she was pregnant. Not only that, she was engaged to be married to a man named Joseph. How would she explain her pregnancy to him? What would she tell her family? What would the elders of her community say?

Now think about what I said in chapter 1 about how uncommon it was for a teenager to be pregnant in the early 1980s. It was even rarer when my mom carried me in the late 1960s. Now think back over two thousand years to when Mary was pregnant. Add the cultural context of being a Hebrew obligated to follow God's moral law and the established order of society. She could have been put to death if she was suspected of sexual sin. But even with that risk, she submitted herself to God's plan.

Though there were surely a few raised eyebrows when the pregnancy began to show, God provided Mary with shelter from shame. First, He proved to Mary the truth of what she had experienced by the revelation of her cousin Elizabeth's pregnancy. Elizabeth's reaction to Mary—and that of Elizabeth's unborn child—reassured Mary that God was with her.

And then there was Joseph, who obviously loved her. The Bible says he planned to end the engagement privately so that Mary would not be put to further shame (Matt. 1:19). God showed him in a dream that Mary was indeed fulfilling His purposes and had not been unfaithful. You know there were some busybodies around that were shocked when Joseph did not end the engagement. They probably accused him of having sexual relations with Mary. I can imagine that they were subjected to a lot of questions from the elders of their people.

But through it all, God proved that He had Mary, Joseph, and the unborn Jesus covered. He later used Joseph to shield the child and Mary from those that sought to destroy Jesus.

And He will provide a shield for you as well. Mary was chosen to fulfill prophecy and to birth the Son of God into the earth. In a similar manner, you are chosen to fulfill the purposes of God and reproduce Christ on the earth. Though this election may lead to moments when people doubt your sanity and question your integrity (remember Job?), the Lord will provide validation and protection.

After Jesus was born, the Lord God confirmed and revealed His presence as the Son of God by angelic message to the shepherds and celestial notice to the magi. As Mary pondered these things in her heart (Luke 2:19), I'll bet she said the shame and embarrassment was nothing compared to the knowledge that she had given birth to the Son of God—the Savior of the world—and fulfilled God's plan for her life.

When you reach the place where you know the purpose and plan of God has been birthed out of you, the momentary shame you have gone through will be worth it all. Trust me; I feel the weight of shame lifting off me even as I write this book. It proves out the words of 2 Corinthians 4:17: "For our light affliction, which is but for a moment, worketh for us a far more exceeding and eternal weight of glory."

Go Get Your Wife!

The prophet Hosea was another person who endured shame for a purpose. Hosea's wife, Gomer, was a harlot—a prostitute—who he had been commanded to take as a wife (not her specifically, but he was instructed to marry a "wife of whoredom"). See Hosea 1:2. She frequently left home to be with other men. Rather than feeling sorry for Hosea and telling him to divorce Gomer so that he could be a better prophet, God told Hosea to go find her! Not only that, he was to buy her back from whomever she was with. Yes, you heard it—God told the man to pay for his own wife!

It gets even better. Hosea was instructed to make love to this woman and to have children with her. He was given specific instruction concerning their names. The children's names were symbolic of the state of God's people. All of this was to illustrate God's relationship with Israel and His love for them despite their unfaithfulness to Him.

What about you? Can God use your jacked-up relationship for His glory? Can you demonstrate the love of God in the midst of your situation? Can you endure in order to show others that God can heal and restore relationships? I know firsthand that it is not easy, but I also know that it can be done. I would tell you my story right now (yes, I have another one), but it is reserved for another chapter. I have a better story for you right now.

Let Him Be Crucified!

The prime example of purposeful shame is the Lord Jesus Christ. Can you imagine the scene in Jerusalem before His crucifixion? If you're having trouble, just indulge me for a moment:

The cry rang out from among the people—the same people Jesus healed, fed, and taught. "Crucify Him!" But Pilate was trying to release Him! Jesus knew this, yet He did or said nothing that would aid Pilate's attempts. Pilate was under strain. His wife had told him not to bother with this man of righteousness. She said her dreams had been troubled because of Him!

Jesus just stood there, giving the most minimal but powerful answers to Pilate's questions. Pilate knew he had to act—the people were thirsty for blood. But did it have to be this man's blood? In a last-ditch effort to save the Galilean, Pilate addressed the people. Surely they would want to see the murderer Barabbas crucified rather than this man!

But, alas, the people had another plan. The Bible tells us that when given the option of which prisoner should be released, they cried out for Barabbas. Moreover, when asked about Jesus, they shouted, "Let Him be crucified!" (Matt. 27:22) Pilate was stunned—he washed his hands of the whole affair after delivering a stern warning. Pilate told the Jews he would not be called to account for the blood of this man.

The Jews, however, responded with a statement that has puzzled me for some time. They said, "Let His blood be on us and on our children!" (Matt. 27:25) Why would they curse their children with the consequences of their actions? I still do not really understand, but I submit it is something to think about: are the seasons of shame our children experience brought about because of our actions? Maybe.

But that's not the point of this narrative. The point is Jesus knew He would be crucified. He explained to His disciples that He would be lifted up the same way Moses lifted up the serpent in the wilderness so that multitudes would be healed (John 3:14). Jesus knew that He had to die. It was the reason that He came into the world.

But such a death! He was humiliated—stripped, mocked, spit upon, beaten, and then crucified. He was publicly destroyed (from a human standpoint), but He understood that it was all for the purpose of reconciling man to God.

Does that mean that it was easy? No! It is not easy to bear the cross. It is not easy to fulfill God's purposes. Knowing that you are obeying God's will does not necessarily allow you to breeze through the process. Jesus prayed! He truly prayed asking God to let this particular cup pass from Him if there was any other way God's purpose could be accomplished (Matt. 26:39, Luke 22:42).

But after He let God know how He felt about what He was going to have to go through, Jesus uttered a sentence that has become another part of my daily prayer, "Nevertheless, not my will, but thy will be done" (Matt. 26:39, Mark 14:30, Luke 22:42). That is a hard prayer to pray, but if you can get to that stage, you can walk through your season of shame without batting an eye. As long as you know that what you are going through is to accomplish the will of God, you will be able to handle it.

The writer of Hebrews, speaking about our Lord, explains it this way. The Bible encourages us to focus our attention, our gaze, on Jesus, who for the joy that was set before Him, endured the cross, despising the shame (Heb. 12:3). What was the joy set before him? Simply, His joy was found in the fulfillment of God's will and man's reconciliation to God.

Ask any church founder or pioneer; I'm sure they would tell you they had to learn to endure so that they could perform the task God laid on their hearts. Many of them were ridiculed, harassed, and abandoned by friends and family. But the conviction that they were moving in the direction of God's purpose carried them through. He has not changed; He will do the same thing for you.

Have you given any thought to what people might learn about God by watching you walk through your season of shame? I know I didn't—not at first. The revelation of that truth did not come to me until years later. And guess who it came from? Dex—my first husband. He told me years after our divorce that I had been a good wife and that I taught him how to hold his peace instead of arguing and fighting. It had never occurred to me during our trials that he was watching my reaction and learning from me. It turns out that what we went through made us both stronger and better. Additionally, it led me to the place where I am today, walking into my purpose with no fear of the past.

From Jesus's example, we discover the high price that God was willing to pay for our redemption. Christ's picture of sacrificial love should elevate our spirits and reveal to us just how much we are treasured by our Creator. As one of my former pastors used to say, God took what He could not replace and traded it for what He could replace. He could have wiped us out, been done with us, and divorced us, if you will.

But through Hosea, Mary, Jesus, me, and you, people can learn that the love of God is richer, fuller, and deeper than any human love. Now that's purpose!

Survival Strategies

- ❖ Pay attention to red flags in every relationship. They let us know something is off-kilter. Ignoring the red flags or thinking that we have the power to change someone is the easiest way to walk into a shameful situation. We have to trust the Spirit of

God to lead us in everything and back away from any relationship that is not God-honoring.

- ❖ Trust God to bring the right relationships into your life. When we override the promptings of the Spirit, we invite the presence of the enemy into our lives. The Bible tells us not to give the devil an opportunity (Eph. 4:26–27). When we get ahead of God's plans and timing, we give the enemy a foothold.
- ❖ Carry out God's plan for your life, even if it interrupts the plans you made for yourself. One of the hardest things to do is face the fact that your plans may not be what God wants for you. We have to be willing to surrender everything to the Lord, knowing that He will give us far greater than what we are longing to hold on to.
- ❖ Pray for God's will to be done in your life. We have to lay our will aside for the sake of God's call upon our lives. This level of sacrifice can only be achieved through prayer. Jesus had to seek God; why won't we?
- ❖ Accept what God allows. Nothing catches God by surprise. He is fully aware of what we are going through. Not only that, He knows the part we usually don't—the *why*. If God has allowed a situation, we have to trust Him to resolve it instead of fighting in our own strength.

3

You're Anointed in Each Season

> The Spirit of the Lord is on me, because he has anointed me to preach good news to the poor. He has sent me to proclaim freedom for the prisoners and recovery of sight for the blind, to release the oppressed, to proclaim the year of the Lord's favor.
>
> —Luke 4:18–19

I TOLD YOU the dramatic story of my marriage to Dex. This chapter begins with the end of that particular drama. In 1997, we separated shortly following my twenty-ninth birthday (there was drama leading up to the separation, but that will probably be another book). The funny thing about our separation was that we spent more time together at that time than we did when we lived in the same house. He would come to my workplace and take me to lunch, and we would sit and talk like everything was going to be cool one day.

Not only that, we still went to church together. I accompanied him on his speaking engagements, and he went with me to mine. We were still intimate sexually and, I thought, emotionally. I figured we were working things out. This lasted about nine months.

Because I thought everything was going to be worked out (I really wanted that), I spent all of the savings I had managed to accumulate on a marriage retreat the weekend of our third anniversary in April 1998. I'll never forget the title: "A Weekend to Remember." (See, it worked!) The retreat was held at a local hotel, and we got a nice room and went there together to strengthen our marriage and see if it could be saved.

The retreat was informative and fun; it had a lot of activities designed to enhance communication between husband and wife, including workshops for each, combined workshops, and a mandatory date night. We did it all! During those two-and-a-half days, we really talked like we hadn't during most of our marriage. We even prayed and cried together, apologizing to one another for all of the hurt and pain.

After the retreat was over, we went our separate ways and returned to business as usual. We still spent time together, but I began to notice more and more evidence of another woman's presence in his life. I looked through his planner one day and saw that he had many pictures of her, including photos taken at her job. He even had her clothing sizes, down to the underwear!

Anyway, I digress. Despite the other issue, we were still together as far as I was concerned until May 17, 1998, the fateful day which changed my life forever—again.

Dex and I went to the 8:00 a.m. service at our church, and then we went to another church, where he preached a powerful word. At the end of the service, he introduced me to the congregation as his wonderful wife, which sort of shocked me considering our living arrangements. Nevertheless, I stood and waved and greeted the people after service with all the smiles and grins I had available.

We went to eat after church, and then we went back to our house. I don't think I want to go into details about what happened there; just believe we acted like we were happily married.

A few hours later, I returned to the bare apartment I was living in. Not long after I got there, my telephone rang. It was my husband, and I could not understand the hesitant tone of his voice.

He said, "I need to tell you something." I should have known better than to ask, but of course I didn't know any better. I said, "What is it?" I can guarantee you that of all the things I thought he might say, what actually came out was nowhere in my line of thinking.

He said to me, "I filed for divorce." Then I said, "What?" But then he finished the sentence: "And it was final about two weeks ago." I am still blown away when I think about it, but nothing can compare to that moment when time stood still for me in an apartment in southwest Houston.

I was so stunned you would have thought that he had reached through the phone and slapped me, and in a way, that is exactly what happened. I didn't know what to say, so like a dummy, I said, "Okay." Then I just hung up the phone, lay down, and started crying. If it was possible to cry a river, I would have done it that day. I must have cried for hours.

Once I stopped crying, I thought, *I need a new church home.* I know, you're thinking to yourself, *This chick is nuts. Her whole life was snatched away, and she's worried about where to go to church?* Yes, I was, because I knew I couldn't go back to where he was. I didn't have it in me.

I called our pastor that night and said, "I need a new church home, Dex divorced me." You would have thought it happened to him. He was so quiet that I thought he had hung up on me. Finally he said, "I thought you two were working things out." I answered, "That's what I thought too. He says the divorce was final two weeks ago." So the pastor said, "I'm going to have to investigate this. I'll call you back. In the meantime, you can come over to [the other church he served as a pastor]."

That Wednesday night, I went to the other church for Bible study. When I walked in, I felt as if a spotlight turned on me, and everyone was looking. I'm sure they weren't, but I was so focused on my issues that I wasn't thinking clearly. In my mind, I could hear the questions: What's she doing here without her husband? Why does she look like she's been crying? Why is the pastor showing her so much attention?

You see, my husband (I guess former husband) and I had been to that church on several occasions. I had been in the denominational choir with several of the members and even served alongside some of them in various ministry endeavors. So they knew me, but really only as part of Elder and Mrs. Johnson. But that part of my life, unbeknownst to them, was over. After church, many of the members asked how he was doing, and I just said that he was fine because, for all I knew, he was. I really hoped he was dead or at least suffering for treating me the way he did, but all I could say was, "He's fine."

I knew that night that I could not go back there. I was devastated at the thought. The house of God had been my refuge since I was seventeen years old. Now I was spiritually homeless and hopelessly embarrassed. I couldn't go back to the church I left when I married him. I couldn't go to church with him, and I couldn't go to the other church without him. I didn't know what to do.

But God had a plan. The Friday after I learned of my divorce, I was moping around my apartment when a friend called me up. She wanted to know what I was doing the next day. I told her I didn't have anything to do since my life was over.

Well you know she asked me, "What are you talking about?" So I said, "Dex divorced me. It was final two weeks ago, he said, and he just told me on Sunday." Again there was a moment of silence that made me think I had lost the call. Then she said, "I am so sorry to hear that. We will be praying for you and for him. Listen, we are doing a street service tomorrow. You should come out and be with us. It will take your mind off this problem. You will be blessed."

I'm thinking, *Didn't she hear me? I'm divorced! I can't minister to anybody! I'm no good! My husband just dumped me like yesterday's garbage, and she's talking to me about ministry. No way!* But all I managed to say was, "I'll see if I can make it."

She told me the place and time and who else was scheduled to be there, and I hung up with no intention of going. Then I started thinking, *I'll go, but I won't say anything.* Then I thought, *Maybe I can help pass out tracts or something.* She had planted a seed in me that got me thinking that maybe there was still some value left in me, although I was sure it couldn't be much. How great could a woman be when her own husband would look her in the face every day while filing divorce papers behind her back?

When I got up on Saturday, I took my time getting dressed. I finally decided to go to the street service to see what was going on. When I got there, my friend, her husband, the pastors from the church she attended, and some of their members were preaching and distributing clothes. I was familiar with the pastor and his wife because they had also been affiliated with my former pastor and the denomination I worshipped with.

You know what happened. As soon as I got there, people started asking me about him. "How is your husband?" So I told the truth. "I have no husband." There must have been something about the way I said it because I got a few strange looks, but people kind of left me alone for a while.

Finally, the pastor called me over and said, "Take this microphone and speak to the people." I was like, "No. I can't. I don't have anything to say." But he was persistent. He said, "Well at least sing something." (Back then, I was a pretty good singer.) So I sang, but when I was finished, he wouldn't take the microphone back. He insisted that I had something to say.

Well, I don't remember what it was, but it turns out that I had about forty-five minutes worth of something to say! People came out of their homes to listen, and some came over to receive prayer and to find out what we were doing.

Before we finished the service, the pastor came and asked me what was going on. I told him I was divorced and spiritually homeless. He said, "I'll be your pastor," and he and his wife gave me the good old right hand of fellowship right there on the street corner. I spent the next eleven years as part of their ministry and served the ministry in many capacities from day 1.

When I called my other pastor and told him I was going to leave, he asked me where I was going. When I told him who my new pastor would be, he said, "That is an excellent choice. Your soul will be well cared for." He also told me to let him know if I needed anything. That let me know that even though things had not gone well, the pastor still thought there was value left in me and believed I could be of service to my new leaders.

The funny thing about it is that Dex and I had often talked about visiting and possibly joining that very same church I joined on that street corner. We just never got around to it. I used to wonder if we could have salvaged our marriage if we had made that move, but now I know it does not matter. The providence of God worked everything out for me, just like His word promises.

At the writing of these pages, it has been over eleven years since the events I've described. The first few weeks were unbearable. I went to work depressed and angry. Sometimes I would start crying in the middle of the day and just have to leave my desk. I bless God that I had a friend in Christ who prayed me through those days. All I had to do was call her and say, "Meet me in the bathroom," and she was there, armed and ready for battle. Anna stood with me and for me when I couldn't stand for myself. She never let the fact that we worked for the government stop her from ministering to me in my time of need.

This woman of God, the friend that invited me to the street service, and my pastor's wife became my sanity during the months it took my soul to recover from hurt and shame. I was upset and depressed many days, but I still served the Lord. I ministered to the best of my ability, but I had no confidence in that ability. I was too ashamed of the way I had been discarded. I just knew that everyone we fellowshipped with knew all about it.

When Dex got married just five short months later, I was even more embarrassed. I thought, *I must not have been important to him at all if I could be so easily replaced.* The enemy tried to drive me out of my mind with feelings of inadequacy and low self-esteem. Sometimes, it seemed like it was working. I fell into sin, seeking approval and validation through sex—child of God and all. I was lost in trying to regain some sense of significance in my life. It seemed as though I was caught in a vicious cycle of trying to prove myself to God and people, failing all the while. Eventually, I had to be delivered all over again.

Then when Dex called me to tell me his new wife was pregnant, I almost died. I used to think that's why he told me, so I could really lose it, but I know now that was only my view of the situation. Fertility was a sensitive issue for me. I have had female problems most of my life. God blessed me with my daughter, but I had never been able to conceive another child. It was one of the things that put a strain on our marriage. I had prayed and asked God to give me a child before I turned thirty, but He did not see fit to do so. I am sure now that He knew what was ahead and made sure to limit the amount of suffering I would endure.

By now you are probably asking yourself, "Why is she telling us all of this?" The answer is simple: I want you to know that no matter how low life takes you, there is still anointing inside of you. You are a treasure that God has placed in the earth, and the fires you go through just make you shine brighter when you come out of them.

The Word of God bears this out. Consider that most of the characters in God's cast had to deal with some hard blows in life. But God always used their suffering to affect a greater glory.

Call Me Bitter

When I think about hard blows, Naomi immediately comes to mind. She, her husband, and their two sons fled from

Bethlehem during a famine (Ruth 1:1–2). They took up residence in the land of Moab and began to settle in there. But just when life was shifting into coasting gear, tragedy struck.

Naomi's husband died. The Bible doesn't tell us how long the family had been in Moab at that time or how he died. It just lets us know that her husband, Elimelech, died and left Naomi with only her two sons for support.

Eventually, Naomi's sons married Moabite women, Orpah and Ruth. Although we are not told initially, we find out later that Ruth was married to Mahlon (Ruth 4:10). Both women likely had family and friends in the general area where they resided with their husbands.

Naomi should have been able to live out the rest of her days provided for by her sons. Perhaps she looked forward to having grandchildren to nurture. But this was not to be. After they had lived in Moab for about ten years, both of Naomi's sons died. Again, we are not told how, but it does not matter. Suddenly, instead of one widow, there are three of them. Three women left without support or provision. Three women without protection.

Apparently, Naomi spent a lot of time thinking about her situation. She decided that it was time for her to go home. The way I imagine it, she weighed all of her options and saw the journey back to Bethlehem as her only real choice.

Having reached this conclusion, Naomi did something that tells you a lot about her heart toward her daughters-in-law and tells you something about those two women as well. Naomi called a meeting with her daughters-in-law in which she released them from all responsibility toward her and her deceased sons. She encouraged the young ladies to return to their people, where they might be able to remarry and live out the rest of their lives in happiness. She wanted them to be free to move on.

What I found interesting is that the daughters-in-law had apparently been taught the Israelites' customs (see Deut. 25:5–6) because Naomi specifically stated that even if she were to marry and have other sons, the daughters-in-law would be old before the sons were of marrying age.

Another thing I found interesting is that both of the daughters-in-law were reluctant to leave Naomi. They were very different from today's society where people marry a spouse while divorcing his or her family from the picture at the very beginning of the relationship. They don't want to be bothered with in-laws while the spouse is alive, much less after the spouse is gone! But Ruth and Orpah were different. These two women had genuine love for Naomi and wanted to stay with her.

Naomi, not knowing how she would be living when she returned home, again urged the ladies to return to their familiar environs. Finally, Orpah began to see the wisdom of Naomi's plan. She gave Naomi her final love hugs and said good-bye.

On the other hand, Ruth's tenacity was even greater than Naomi's. Ruth pleaded with her. She said, "Don't ask me to leave you" (Ruth 1:16). Her plea to accompany Naomi is one of the most beautiful examples of human devotion found in the Scripture. In fact, it is so profound that many people use it as part of their wedding vows (I did when I remarried in 2005). I am going to share it with you so that you can feel Ruth's heart on this issue:

> Do not persuade me to leave you or go back and not follow you. For wherever you go, I will go, and wherever you live, I will live; your people will be my people and your God will be my God. Where you die, I will die, and there I will be buried. May the Lord do this to me, and even more, if anything but death separates you and me. (Ruth 1:16–17, HCSB)

Ruth was willing to take a big chance by going with Naomi into parts unknown. One would think that would convince Naomi of her worth, but like many of us, she was focused on what had gone wrong in her life. When she and Ruth arrived in Bethlehem, many were excited to see her. But again, like many of us, she put a damper on their excitement. Instead of being encouraged by the fact that people were happy to see her, she began to sing her sad song.

I'm going to paraphrase her lament: "Don't even call me Naomi anymore. All I am now is bitter—I don't know why God has been so hard on me—call me Mara." Mara, you see, meant "bitter." Life had been so harsh in Naomi's eyes that she wanted to change her name so that everyone would know it. She had lost sight of the fact that God has a plan even when we don't (see Ruth 1:20–22 for Naomi's whole statement).

Naomi is not alone. Many of us forget that God has ways that we cannot understand with our human minds. We usually forget not when things are well with us, but when things begin to go wrong. Didn't I tell you that just because of what happened in my marriage I felt like my life was over? Have you ever felt that way? If you have, or even if you do right now, it's all right. The Lord knows how we feel. He understands our human emotions; as a matter of fact, He created them. So He does not condemn us for feeling this way. But He does not want us to stay down in the dumps and depressed. As I have heard it said, "It is one thing to fall and another thing to wallow."

Do you know the difference? Wallowing is what happens when we fall, and instead of getting up, we lie down in the dirt and roll over and over, covering ourselves in filth. God does not mind us falling; He does, however, have an issue when we choose to wallow. He wants us to trust Him to help us recover from every adverse situation in our lives. You can—you must—get up again!

Now let's get back to Naomi. She eventually worked her way back into society. Instead of sitting in a corner and wasting away, she got busy. And it was all because of Ruth. You see, Naomi's concern for Ruth was greater than her despair over her own situation. She wanted to make sure that Ruth was taken care of. So she got involved in Ruth's day-to-day affairs, giving her wise counsel about securing the attention of Boaz (Ruth 3:1–4).

Ruth followed Naomi's advice and became Boaz's wife, securing a place in the lineage of King David and of the Lord Jesus Christ. What was interesting to me is what the women said when Ruth gave birth to her baby, Obed.

The women who gathered at Obed's birth didn't talk about how blessed Ruth was to have gotten such a fine husband and child; rather, they ascribed the blessings to Naomi:

> And the women said unto Naomi, Blessed [be] the LORD, which hath not left thee this day without a kinsman, that his name may be famous in Israel. And he shall be unto thee a restorer of [thy] life, and a nourisher of thine old age: for thy daughter in law, which loveth thee, which is better to thee than seven sons, hath born him. And Naomi took

the child, and laid it in her bosom, and became nurse unto it. And the women her neighbours gave it a name, saying, There is a son born to Naomi; and they called his name Obed: he [is] the father of Jesse, the father of David. (Ruth 4:14–17, KJV)

Isn't that powerful? God left it on record: no matter what your circumstances are, He has an answer. He can restore anything that you lose. No need to be bitter. The key is to take the focus off yourself and be concerned about someone else. Allow God to show you who is in need of the particular skills and abilities He has given you. And finally, allow Him to bless you through your blessing of others.

My loss was not nearly as devastating as Naomi's, but I felt just as hurt and bitter as I imagine she did for a while. However, as much as I wanted to give up, I still had a reason to live: my daughter. She was still in high school, and this mess I was in had nothing to do with her. So I prayed and cried when I needed to, but I also set about making the best life I could for her. We had lost our material security, but I believed that the Lord would see us through. I bought a brand-new car for the first time (I never thought I could do it, so I had never tried), we moved from our "divorce recovery" one-bedroom apartment into a nice two-bedroom, and we went on with life. A new job opportunity came to me the same year as my divorce, and for the first time, I had no trouble moving out of my comfort zone to try a totally new field of work. I made the decision to step out and do what I could to increase my income so that my child and I would have a better quality of life. Loss proved to be the catalyst to a better life for us in many ways. I began to learn to depend on God instead of depending on people for safety and security.

Also, having a new church home proved to be a blessing for me as well. I had been doing some speaking at events and sang in various choirs, but in my new church home, God opened doors for a variety of ministry. I was able to minister to and teach children, youth, and adults, hone my skills at desktop publishing, learn to praise dance, and much more. Spending time in the evangelistic ministry helped me to take my focus off my problems and reach out to others who were hurting. Remembering the fact that Jesus had not left me, I found a hope and a courage that I was able to share with others, encouraging them to step out and try new things. Instead of being bitter, I can look back and say that I became better through my season of shame. Having others to focus on helped me to avoid self-pity and apply the energy I would have wasted wallowing to helping people. Don't get me wrong; change did not come overnight. Recovering from shame was a long process, but having challenging work to do helped me keep going every time I wanted to quit.

The Child Shall Not Live

When you think about it, you note that the Bible is full of survival stories. You should take the time to read it. Many of the families are utterly dysfunctional, yet someone in the family is always used to fulfill God's purposes. That should serve as a great encouragement to you.

In this segment, I want to talk about the king of Israel, the sweet psalmist David. Many people are familiar with the story of David and Goliath and how David killed that formidable giant. We use his success to make us feel that no matter how small we are, we still have a chance against much larger opponents when we face them with God's help.

But David's victory over Goliath is only a small part of his story. There is another segment that gets our attention for this book. Once David's kingdom was solidified and his reign established by God and accepted by the people, he began to be at ease. The Bible says this particular incident started at the time that kings normally go to war. But David did not go to war; he sent his men and stayed in the palace (2 Sam. 11:1).

One day as he was relaxing at home, he noticed a woman bathing herself on a rooftop. The Bible doesn't tell us much about her other than that she was beautiful; she caught David's eye and stirred his desire. He took her into the palace and had sex with her, then he sent her back home.

This woman was married, but David disregarded that fact in order to quench his thirst for her. I'm sure he thought no one would be the wiser, and since he was the king, he could probably buy her silence with a few gifts. But as Moses said, "Be sure your sin will find you out" (Num. 32:23b).

The woman, Bathsheba, became pregnant. Eventually she sent word of her pregnancy to David. His response was very calculated; instead of simply denying paternity, he set about covering things up.

He called Bathsheba's husband, Uriah the Hittite, away from the army and tried to convince him to go home and sleep with his wife. He must have thought that the timing would be close enough for her to pass off his child as Uriah's. But Uriah himself threw a monkey wrench into those works. Instead of being grateful for the reprieve from war, he refused to go home and be comfortable while his fellow soldiers were fighting for their lives! Two times David encouraged Uriah to go home, and two times Uriah chose not to go.

Foiled by Uriah's loyalty, David hatched another plan. He sent Uriah back to the army with a message for the commander. The message was to put Uriah on the front line in the heat of battle and then draw back so that he would be killed. And that is exactly what happened. (See 2 Sam. 11:14–16). Once Uriah was dead, and an appropriate time had passed, David sent for Bathsheba and made her one of his wives. But as I often say, God is not asleep. He watched it all unfold. Not surprisingly, the Bible says that what David did displeased the Lord (2 Sam. 11:27).

God sent word to David through Nathan the prophet. I love the way Nathan dealt with David. He used such wisdom! He didn't just walk in and denounce David's actions; instead, he told him a story. You can read the whole story in 2 Samuel 11–12. I just had to set the stage. But the dramatic conclusion, at least in my eyes, was the pronouncement that the child born through this sin would not live (2 Sam. 12:14).

I couldn't understand that. Why, in this scenario, did death come to the two people who were completely innocent? Bad enough Uriah was murdered; now the child who had done no wrong had to die as well. God said so. Many of us spend a lot of time dwelling on events in our lives that we view as unfair. But this—wow!

Even more remarkable than the events I've already described is David's response. He repented right away. You can read his beautiful prayer of repentance in Psalm 51. But he also mourned and interceded on his son's behalf. You see, David remembered something that many of us forget when we face life's hard situations, especially those we bring upon ourselves: God is not only just, He is merciful. David was smart enough to go before God and appeal to His mercy. Only this time, it didn't work. God indeed let the child die.

David refused to eat and prostrated himself before the Lord for the life of his child. Once he found out the child had died, he rose up and ate, then resumed his position as king. He did not fold up and let the shame of what he had done take over. He remembered that despite his failures, he was the Lord's anointed. He knew that his fulfillment of God's purposes was greater than any personal tragedy.

This is a lesson that we all need to learn: our mistakes do not negate God's anointing. We have to repent, turn away from sin, get up, and get back into position. God's purposes are greater than our mistakes, and if He chooses to use us in spite of our failures, we have to trust Him to carry us through.

Just like my friends encouraged me to use my God-given gifts even in the midst of the greatest crisis I had ever faced, I want to encourage you right now to know that this—yes, even this—is part of God's plan to make you exactly what He wants you to be. It doesn't matter how you have failed, how you have been hurt, or who talks behind your back or in your face; the Lord has need of you! And as you acknowledge your anointing, your season of shame loses the strength to hold you down.

Survival Strategies

- ❖ Repent immediately of any sin in your life and turn away from it! The longer we persist in sin, the greater the stronghold the enemy can have in our lives. We have the promise of forgiveness when we confess, but if we attempt to cover our sins, we will not get ahead.
- ❖ Do not try to hide anything from God—fears, failures, disappointments. Confess them to Him. It's not like we can hide from God anyway; He is all-knowing. The Holy Spirit is living inside of us if we are believers in Jesus Christ. He is aware of what we are feeling and wants us to come to Him with our issues. After all, He is the only One who can handle them!
- ❖ Remember that you were born for a purpose and that God is able to bring that purpose to pass! There are many great resources to help us discover our purpose, but the best one of all is the Bible itself. We have to search its pages in order to find the meaning for our lives.
- ❖ Ask God for His mercy when needed, but don't give up hope if He doesn't erase sin's consequences. The grace of God is sufficient to carry us in the aftermath of our folly.

4

Praise God in the Season

> Be joyful always; pray continually; give thanks in
> all circumstances, for this is God's will for you in
> Christ Jesus.
>
> —1 Thessalonians 5:16–18

I'VE GOT TO admit, I've told you way more about my life than I ever wanted to. But I need to let you know that I understand the persistent power of shame. This book is not about me, per se, but it is my book, my gift to you, so that you can overcome your season and move forward with your life.

This part of the story is very fresh, occurring not very long ago. In fact, the struggle to overcome it is ongoing. It is also very personal, but I am telling you because it is also very powerful.

My husband, Darryl, is an absolute jewel. He loves me without question and has been pushing me to finish this book. I talked to him about this particular chapter before I decided to write it because it involves him as much as it involves me. He said it was okay to tell you, so I will—not every detail, but that which is relevant to the subject.

We met at church a few years before we actually formed a relationship. His mother, sister, and nieces were all members of the church; his mother and sister were raising the girls, and I greatly admired that. But Brother Darryl was another story. He was friendly enough, but I knew that he had been in trouble at some point in the past, and I wanted no part of that. I spent a lot of time worrying about my security. I was scared about my job, my future—everything.

After my divorce, I also got scared every time I thought someone was looking at me. Don't get me wrong; I tried my share of relationships with men. But they never seemed to work out because I was seeking relationships for the wrong reasons. Time after time, one thing lead to another, and then everything fell apart. So I had finally given up trying to be with someone, thinking that God intended me to live out the rest of my days alone.

Anyway, after a few years, Brother Darryl started speaking to me all the time. He never said a lot, but he always made sure to say something. I always answered him, but I must confess I was not always the saint I should have been. I acted smug and self-righteous—as if I didn't want to be bothered with him. After all, I was a minister, an ordained evangelist of the church, and it would not do for me to be giving a man too much attention.

At the end of 2004, completely out of the blue, Brother Darryl asked me if he could call me sometime. I was surprised, but I said yes. We began to talk on the phone daily, and I discovered that I actually liked him. He was attentive and caring. He made me laugh, and he always encouraged me to express my thoughts and feelings.

Soon we were spending a lot of time together. He would come to my house, and we would watch television together. He even endeared himself to my daughter because of his devotion to my grandson, who was only a few months old when we began to see each other.

Well, we married in October 2005 and began our life together. My daughter thought he was all right (her words), and my grandson loved him. He was a hit with my family, which is a hard thing to be. It seemed that all was well.

Gradually we began to notice that things were missing around the house. It was little things at first—DVDs, CDs, and things of that nature—but it started happening more and more often. My daughter tried to tell me that it was Darryl taking things out of the house, but I was so overwhelmed by other things that were happening (I had contracted a serious staph infection and was dealing with that) that I basically denied it all.

When we moved into our house in May 2006, Darryl spearheaded the move. Some of the things we had in the apartment never made it to our new home. I was furious! But not really understanding what was happening, I talked to him about it, believed his promises that it wouldn't happen again, and carried on with life.

Well it happened again and again, to the point that my daughter decided to move out and get her own place. I could not understand it. How did this wonderful man turn into a nightmare? I began to question him constantly about everything he said and did. He assured me that he would get his problem (which he said was gambling) under control. Because I loved him, I believed it.

The story could be much longer, but I am sure I have said enough. You get the picture, so I won't go into every detail. What I will tell you is that it got so bad that he began taking money from our joint bank account. That threw our new mortgage into arrears, and I wound up borrowing money from a friend just to stay afloat. I typed up divorce papers because I felt betrayed and abused. I did not get married to go through all that! After one incident that occurred while I was out of town on business, I threatened to kill him—and I meant it too!

Surviving Your Season of Shame

But God did not allow me to commit homicide; in fact, He made sure I didn't by allowing my pastor to intervene before I got back to Houston. After much discussion, we agreed that it would be best for Darryl to go to rehab. You see, he confessed to our pastor and a trusted friend that he actually had a problem with drugs. One of our minister friends was connected to several recovery homes, and sensing that it would be unwise for him to remain in the local area, he drove Darryl to San Antonio to participate in a treatment program. He stayed for three months.

My husband returned home, and everything was good—dare I say it again?—for a while. After about a year, the telltale signs of addiction began to creep into our lives again. At one point he actually left and stayed gone for nearly forty days. I filed a missing person's report with the local sheriff's department and prayed that he had not been killed somewhere. I had come to the point where I didn't really want him back; I just didn't want anything bad to happen to him on my watch.

One of Darryl's nieces just would not give up on him. She went and found where he was and brought him back to his mother's home. After a while, he came back home to me. After much prayer and discussion, Darryl wound up going back to San Antonio to a different recovery home. This time he stayed a year. Those people filled him with love and with the Bible! My grandson and I made several trips to visit him, and he was even allowed to come home for one holiday. Finally, we began to see real progress. After the year was over, he came home, and we determined to start over again.

However, recovery is a process, and sometimes, it is slow. Darryl began to drift back into the same behavior of the past. It became so troublesome that I told him not to come back home. He was over at his mother's, wrestling with his addiction, when he decided to go through the recovery process again. He went to Amarillo, Texas, this time and submitted to the leadership of the former home director from the San Antonio recovery home. By the way, if you or someone you know needs help with recovery, Victory Outreach has free recovery homes all over the world. Visit www.victoryoutreach.org for more information.

Darryl has since come home, and we are moving forward. I'm not saying it is all gravy, but we are healing, trusting, and loving once again. He is my greatest supporter and part of the reason that I am even working on this book right now. In spite of everything that we have been through—or possibly because of it—we are more determined to do what the Lord wants of us as a team and individually.

What I want you to get from this story is that life continues to move on. While all of this was happening, I still had to go to work. I still had to be a mother, grandmother, daughter, sister, wife, friend, and minister. You better believe it was not easy. Some of the people I thought were with me talked behind my back—some of them talked to my face! I cried many tears and prayed many self-pitying prayers. Despite what I was going through, I still had to trust God for the outcome and praise Him in the meantime just like some of my favorite Bible characters.

Married to Nabal

You want to talk about a marriage with some problems, just take a look at Abigail and Nabal. The Bible describes Abigail as beautiful and gracious. But Nabal was a different story. The Bible relates that his name means "fool," and you can tell by the things he did he had no problem living up to his name! You can read the whole story in 1 Samuel 25, but allow me to summarize for you here.

Nabal was a rich man with a lot of possessions, including fields and livestock. As it turns out, his herdsmen found themselves under the watchful care of David and his men while out in the plains with Nabal's flocks. Even though Nabal did not ask for this protection, he did not turn it down either.

When it came time for the sheep to be sheared, Nabal's men went to work. Imagine David and his men, who were literally on the run. I am sure they were hungry and in need of a little generosity. They did not think twice about asking Nabal for a little of what he had. After all, Nabal was rich, and they had done right by him by protecting his things instead of taking them by force or allowing them to be taken by someone else.

Nabal, however, saw the situation a little differently. In his mind, David was an interloper who had intruded upon his doings. He declared he did not care who David was or what he had done; he owed him nothing and would give him nothing! See 1 Samuel 25:10.

Well, as you know, the male species are not usually given to being insulted and doing nothing about it. David was infuriated by Nabal's response and swore that he would kill every male in Nabal's household. He and his men began to gear up to attack the one whose stuff they had once protected.

Fortunately, a wise servant went straight to Abigail with the news. I can imagine the servant screaming, "Your husband is about to get us all killed! You have to do something!" Abigail did not confront Nabal about what had happened; I'm sure she knew it would do no good. After all, she lived with the man and knew exactly who he was. He undoubtedly would have seen her intervention as taking sides against him.

Instead, Abigail quickly sprang into action. She brought provisions for David and his men out of her storehouse, making sure that there was more than enough to meet their needs. In order to smooth things over, Abigail did not send the servants to take care of business alone; she went to address the problem herself.

This woman went directly to David and acknowledged what everyone knew: that he would be king one day. She gave David courtesy and respect that he never would have gotten from Nabal. Abigail was also realistic about her husband and his actions. She did not make excuses; she dealt with things just as they were. Abigail took responsibility for all that had happened and cautioned David against acting rashly. He could not help but recognize her wisdom in the face of a situation that was completely embarrassing to her household.

When Abigail returned home, she found her husband celebrating his abundance in grand fashion, not even knowing or caring that he had put his entire household in jeopardy. Wisely, she did not tell him what she had done; that would have ruined his party for sure! She left him well enough alone until the next day. Then, when Abigail told Nabal what she had done, he reacted just as she probably expected—with a cold anger that eventually killed him (1 Sam. 25:37–39).

After Nabal was gone, David came calling, eventually making Abigail his wife. Her consistency in the face of her season of shame brought her into the household of the king. While events for you may not play out in such a dramatic fashion, a lesson can be learned from Abigail. She was prepared to handle any situation that came her way. In the midst of embarrassment, she kept her head and diffused the situation by calling upon her strengths to deal with both David and Nabal.

Abigail could have ignored the situation or gotten into a dramatic confrontation with Nabal, but she chose to remain steady and deal with the crisis head-on. I believe that if you remain consistent in the midst of your season of shame, God will strengthen and empower you to avert total disaster as well. And who knows? You might just wind up married to a king!

Love Don't Live Here

While we're on the subject of marriages made someplace other than Heaven, let me introduce you to Leah. Leah was married to a man that didn't love her—talk about embarrassing! Let's take a look at how it all went down.

This is a story from the book of Genesis that really gets to you. See chapters 25, 27, 29, and 30 for the full text of the events that I am about to describe.

The central character, Jacob, stole his older brother Esau's birthright (the rights and privileges of the firstborn son) with their mother's help. He also masqueraded as his brother and received the blessing that his father had reserved for Esau. You know Esau was hopping mad! When he determined to take Jacob out, it was good old Mom to the rescue again. She sent Jacob to her brother, Laban, in order to protect him from Esau's wrath.

When Jacob arrived at Uncle Laban's house, he fell madly in love with Laban's daughter, Rachel. Jacob loved her so much that he promised to work for Laban for seven years just so he could marry her! You don't see that kind of devotion much these days, but that is material for another book. Jacob wanted to be with Rachel, to have her as his wife so badly, that the Bible tells us that his years of work felt like nothing to him (Gen. 29:20).

Imagine Jacob's delight when the wedding night finally arrived. All of his hard work had paid off, and he got to claim his bride. I can only speculate, but I would assume that he was very passionate that first night, having the object of his desire at last. Or so he thought.

It turns out Jacob wasn't the only trickster in the family. The Bible says that the next morning, Jacob did not open his eyes to the love of his life but to her older sister, Leah! Laban explained his deceit by telling Jacob that in their culture, the older sister needed to be married before the younger one (Gen. 29:26). So Jacob was bound to Leah through no choice of his own, and he had to continue to work for Laban to get the wife he really wanted.

Now let's turn our thoughts to Leah. The Bible tells us that Rachel was beautiful; no such trait is ascribed to Leah. So here she is, the less-attractive older sister, suddenly married to a man that she knows does not want her. Because of the time she lived in, she was bound by her father's actions and the marriage covenant, but can you even begin to know how she felt knowing that hers was a loveless marriage?

Leah was like many of us. She was preoccupied with her situation and consumed by what she did not have. Until she began to have children, it seemed she was painfully unaware that the Lord was mindful of her plight (Gen. 29:31). You can infer from the Scriptures Leah's desperation to make her husband love her. She bore him three sons, proclaiming with each one, "Now my husband will love me" (Gen. 29:32–34). Time and again it seemed her hopes were dashed. Can you imagine the shame she must have felt? In my mind, I can hear her saying, "Here I am married to this man. It's all Dad's fault! I was fine living at home being unmarried. Stupid traditions! Everybody knows Jacob didn't want me, but he still expects me to give him the privileges of a wife—surrendering my body to him and giving him children! How in the world did this happen to me?"

Or it could be that Leah had been in love with Jacob the whole time, envying the fact that her younger sister, who had no lack of admirers, had gotten a supreme catch! She may have had a momentary sense of triumph when she was the surprise bride, but I'm sure Jacob's reaction killed that right away. Such hidden feelings would explain her insistence that she would make him love her. Leah may have tried to make the best of a bad situation by becoming the ideal wife, accommodating all of her husband's desires. Honestly, we don't know, because we aren't given much of her story prior to the wedding or immediately after.

In any event, after giving birth to Simeon, Ruben, and Levi, Leah was still painfully aware that her husband did not love her. But finally, while pregnant with her fourth son, something shifted inside her. She took the focus off what she did not have and began to focus on a different direction. When her fourth son was born, she named him Judah, which meant "praise." Leah declared, "Now I will praise the Lord" (Gen. 29:35), meaning that in spite of her circumstances remaining the same, she would honor God in the midst of it all.

Much more happened in the story of Jacob, Leah, and Rachel. You can read it for yourself in the book of Genesis. Leah went on to have other sons and a daughter and was the most fruitful of Jacob's wives. You can see from further reading, however, that the rivalry between her and Rachel never really came to an end. That seems to be the way it is with siblings sometimes. But to Jacob's credit, he treated Leah as his wife in every sense of the word, taking care of her and the children, as well as the rest of his household, the rest of his days. In addition, God did something remarkable for Leah although she could not have known it would happen at the time: He designated Judah as the line from which the future line of kings of His people would descend, including our Savior, the Lord Jesus Christ, called the Lion of the tribe of Judah (Rev. 5:5).

What is my point? It is simply this: although the season of shame you are in may seem unbearable, you never know how God is using it to produce something great. You can either spend all your time trying to change the way things are and exhaust yourself concentrating on what you do not have, or you can learn to praise the Lord. This is God's desire for us—that in all things and at all times, we begin to give thanks and trust Him with the outcome of every situation (1 Thess. 5:18).

No Prayer Allowed

Let me turn a corner away from marriage for a moment. A great example of praising God in the midst of a difficult situation is Daniel. His story is relayed in the Bible book bearing his name. A Hebrew brought into captivity by the Babylonians as a youth, Daniel spent most of his life serving foreign kings as a counselor and administrator. He also faithfully served the Lord of his ancestry, who gifted him to interpret dreams.

Daniel's success in the kingdom led to jealousy from his coworkers. They looked for something that they could bring to the king in order to bring Daniel down. The Bible relates that the only thing they could come up with was to accuse him in matters of his religion (Dan. 6:5). You see, throughout history, the Jews were known for their stringent devotion to their God. They were a people who believed and acted differently from all others.

Because Daniel had favor with the king, his enemies had to be subtle in their approach. So instead of talking to the king about Daniel, they boosted the king's ego by telling him that, essentially, he was God, and everybody should have to come to him to make petitions rather than praying to any other deity.

The evil counselors achieved their goal; the king signed a decree stating that if anyone prayed to any god other than him, they would be thrown into a den of lions (Dan. 6:6–9). You can be sure the lions would be prepared to enjoy their meal!

But this is where it gets interesting. The Bible says that when Daniel knew that the order had been made, he kept up his usual practice of praying in an open window three times a day! (Dan. 6:10) Can you imagine that? Many of us would not be so bold. Knowing that a rule specifically designed to entrap us was in place, we would either stop praying for a while until the heat was off, or we would hide in a closet in the most private part of our home.

Daniel continued his devotions because of his relationship with God. He was not worried about what the king was going to do. He knew that God would deal with it. After all, he had seen God work in many ways during his time in the kingdom. He knew God's track record, and his faith remained strong in the face of opposition.

Daniel's rivals could not wait to bring the king the news! I can imagine them pretending to be shocked, feigning humility when reporting to the king about Daniel's activities. "Oh, King, we really don't want to tell you this, but there are people here who don't respect you or your royal decrees. Daniel is one of those people." To make sure the king followed through, they reminded him that decrees made by the king could not be changed (Dan. 6:15). Imagine them. "Oh, King, we know you love Daniel, but the law is the law."

The king was in a pickle! I bet he would have given anything to take back his foolish law. But in order to save face with his subordinates, he had to follow through with the punishment he had decreed: Daniel would have to be cast into the lions' den. The very thought filled the king with grief.

The Bible tells us that when Daniel was cast into the den of lions, the king was the one who offered him encouragement. He said, "May your God, whom you serve continually, deliver you" (Dan. 6:16). All that night, the king couldn't sleep. He rejected food and entertainment and spent the night worrying about Daniel. I bet he prayed to that God he had forbidden others to pray to!

The next morning the king ran to the mouth of the den and called out to Daniel. Imagine his surprise when he heard the reply, "Oh, King, live forever" (Dan. 6:21).

The king was overjoyed! Daniel was alive! But he had to find out how. Daniel's explanation was so simple it must have sounded insane to those around him. "My God sent His angel to shut the lions' mouths." I bet those who were behind the plot were terrified when they heard that. And they should have been.

Once Daniel was pulled out of the lions' den, the king commanded that all Daniel's accusers and their families be thrown in. Deprived of the meal from the previous night, Daniel, the hungry lions pounced on them and tore them to pieces. The king proclaimed the God of Daniel as the only true God. God proved Himself faithful to the one who had proved faithful to Him (Dan. 6:24–27).

Daniel's habit of prayer developed a deep abiding faith that was victorious when put to the test. What about you? Have you developed a consistent relationship with God that will stand the trials of life? Surviving your season of shame requires a steadfast faith that can't be shaken by opposition. You must both pray and believe God for the outcome on a consistent basis.

Jesus taught his disciples that men should always pray, not tiring and not giving up (Luke 18). He understood that constant communication with God prepares you to face any opposition that arises. It strengthens your connection to God and holds you up when it seems that you have nothing to stand on. Prayer is a powerful weapon in our spiritual survival arsenal.

Survival Strategies

- ❖ Allow God to keep you in peace in the midst of your situation. You must know in your heart that deliverance does not always come in the way we have in mind. But it does come! A consistent faith in God leads to a consistent expectation of victory.
- ❖ Demonstrate that peace by fulfilling your responsibilities and remaining consistent. Be your best, and do your best no matter who opposes you. In the end, your excellent spirit will earn you a place of favor. We also demonstrate godly character when we operate in the spirit of excellence.
- ❖ Continue to discipline yourself in the midst of your trials by praying and worshiping God. It is important to stay faithful. In prayer, praise, and worship, we gain the strength we need in order to withstand opposition. Not only that, we please God, and that

causes Him to act on our behalf. When we strive to be close to Him, He comes close to us.

❖ Even if the situation does not change, allow God to change you in the midst of your madness. Sometimes, things don't change. God allows us to be pressed in order for the anointing inside of us to be squeezed out for the benefit of others. He allows us to endure the fiery trials of life in order to purify us. We must trust the Lord to make us better, not bitter, through our experiences.

5

God Restores in Due Season

> Come, let us return to the LORD. He has torn us to pieces but he will heal us; he has injured us but he will bind up our wounds. After two days he will revive us; on the third day he will restore us, that we may live in his presence. Let us acknowledge the LORD; let us press on to acknowledge him. As surely as the sun rises, he will appear; he will come to us like the winter rains, like the spring rains that water the earth.
>
> —Hosea 6:1–3

AS YOU CAN see, a season of shame can begin at any time. Often without warning, you find yourself in the midst of a situation that seems permanently painful. I have experienced such circumstances at home, at school, in the workplace, and even in the church! All of them are filled with the one thing that makes a season of shame inevitable: people, including me and you.

When we are ostracized, criticized, and marginalized, it is easy to give up. The enemy of your soul, the devil, wants you to respond to your season of shame by isolating yourself from people who love you. He wants you to turn away from God. He wants you to believe that you are all alone and that there is no one who cares about what you are facing.

I understand. I have felt all of those feelings and then some. Every now and then, I have been guilty of giving in to those feelings. Let me tell you, cussing and fussing does not solve the problem; they only make it worse. Especially if you call yourself a child of God. The Bible tells us plainly that our human outbursts of anger cannot accomplish the righteousness of God (James 1:19–20). Our hasty actions and drastic overreactions are not God's ideal. We must conduct ourselves well, no matter what season we are in.

Let me encourage you! I have lost houses, cars, relationships, health, and more over the years. I have been divorced once, bankrupt twice, and without a church home more a few times. I was a teenage mother, and I have been a single parent. I dropped out of high school (thank God I went back) and dropped out of college (I haven't finished yet, but I will). Before I got saved, I was a juvenile delinquent and bound for mischief at every turn. But in due season,

God saw fit to save me from my sins. He rescued me from sure destruction and set me on the path that led to where I am today.

God restored my life. He made me a better mother and taught me how to be a wife. He blessed me with two beautiful grandchildren! The house I live in is larger than both of the houses I lost, and I have a better job than I ever thought possible. In spite of the few not-so-pleasant church experiences in my past, I love the Lord and His people. He has anointed me for ministry and given me a great group of people to serve as pastor. As you have read in the pages of this book, my life has not all been easy. But God is bringing me into a new season of life, and I am excited to see what form it is going to take.

Restoration is God's business; we have to let Him handle it. He does so through time and circumstances. Our job is to walk through the process on an even keel. We have to develop the ability to "maintain in the meantime." One of the reasons we need to maintain our composure at all times is because God is faithful. And He has a season for you that does not appear on any calendar.

Because He exists outside of time, He can create a new season whenever He chooses to do so. Eventually, He changes the scenery that you have been seeing on your spiritual journey, just like the scenery changes on a natural road trip. When this unpredictable season—known in the Bible as due season—drops into your life, it puts an immediate end to your season of shame. The Bible encourages us that it will come if you don't lose heart (Gal. 6:7–9). You may not know how or when, but let the following biblical characters encourage you that due season is coming! When it comes, restoration is a part of the package.

Not Child—Children!

The book of 1 Samuel opens with the story of a woman named Hannah. Hannah is married to a devout man named Elkanah, who loves her dearly. But Hannah has two problems, one of which compounds the other. The first problem is that Elkanah has another wife, Peninnah. The second problem is that Hannah is barren—has no children—while Peninnah has plenty. A barren woman was a source of shame in those days.

This situation caused Hannah much grief. She agonized over her childlessness, and nothing her husband said brought her comfort. Peninnah constantly tormented Hannah about her barrenness. Elkanah clearly favored Hannah, but it is likely that neither of them knew what the Bible tells us: God had prevented Hannah from bearing children (1 Sam. 1:6).

Year after year, the family traveled to Shiloh to make the required sacrifices and to worship the Lord. Elkanah made sure to give Hannah a great portion of the sacrifice, but in her mind, nothing could make up for her lack of a child, specifically a son who would carry on the legacy of his father and could possibly be the promised Messiah! Hannah was so grieved by the whole situation that she wept and would not eat.

Poor Elkanah! He couldn't understand what Hannah's issue was. He said to her, "Hannah, why weepest thou? And why eatest thou not? And why is thy heart grieved? Am not I better to thee than ten sons?" (1 Sam. 1:8, KJV) He loved her and didn't want to see her in agony over something over which they had no control.

But Hannah had gotten to her breaking point, and she did what all of us should do when that happens: she began to pray and lay her request before the Lord. The Bible says she was in such agony of soul that when she was praying, no words came out even though her mouth was moving. She made a powerful vow to the Lord, promising that if He gave her a son, she would give him completely over to the Lord's service (1 Sam. 1:11).

Hannah prayed so fervently that the old priest, Eli, who was watching her, thought she was drunk. She was out of it! But she was completely into it as well, praying her heart out with no idea that she was being watched. When Eli confronted her and accused her of being drunk, Hannah was nonplussed. She told him that she had poured out her soul to the Lord; she was not a worthless woman with no better sense than to be drunk in the temple!

When Eli heard that, his heart apparently softened toward Hannah's plight. He sent her away with a blessing, praying that the Lord would grant her request (1 Sam. 1:17). Hannah went away encouraged.

And God gave her what she asked for! Hannah had a son and named him Samuel, which means "asked of God." She weaned him and then took him to the priest Eli to be raised in the temple in the Lord's service. She made sure the priest knew that the son she was presenting to the Lord was the answer to her anguished prayer. God granted her petition, and Hannah kept her vow. She was not like most people who forget God when they get what they want from Him.

The Bible says that Hannah prepared a garment for Samuel every year and took it to him when the family went to Shiloh for worship (1 Sam. 2:19). So she maintained a relationship with her son, continuing to nurture him. But even greater, God honored Hannah's sacrifice of her firstborn son (sound familiar?) and blessed her to have five more children—three sons and two daughters (1 Sam. 1:21). She went from desperate for a child to being a mother of children! Her experience was reflective of the words of Psalm 113:9, "He maketh the barren woman to keep house, and to be a joyful mother of children. Praise ye the LORD."

Hannah's motherhood erased the stigma of her barrenness. Her firstborn, Samuel, went on to become the last of the judges of Israel. He served as a priest and prophet of the Lord for the rest of his days. It was Samuel who heard God's voice and warned Eli of God's judgment concerning his family. It was Samuel who anointed Israel's first and second kings, Saul and David, respectively. I'm sure Hannah did not have all of that in mind when she prayed her agonized prayer, but God looked on her need, saw her heart for Him, and used her to bring about a regime change among His people. Now that is restoration.

More Than Before

Speaking of restoration, let's go back to Job—remember him from the first chapter? We talked about his many terrible losses and the remarkable attitude that he displayed in the midst of his trouble, but here we get to explore the rest of the story.

In the book bearing his name, Job spent a lot of time discoursing with his friends about the source of his troubles and the meaning of life. He held on to his integrity and was careful not to blame God even though he did not understand what he was going through. He tried to reason it out, but eventually, he found himself face-to-face with his Creator.

God confronted Job and his friends with a series of questions about the origins of the universe and life itself that they could not possibly answer. He let them know that He did not need their advice when the world was created, and He certainly did not need it in Job's situation. It was through this exchange that Job realized that he was just really finding out who God was. He said, "I have heard of thee by the hearing of the ear: but now mine eye seeth thee. Wherefore I abhor myself, and repent in dust and ashes" (Job 42:5–6, KJV). That was one part of Job's restoration; he went from a ritual understanding of God to repentance. Job's repentance led to him having an authentic and truly personal relationship with God.

But that is not all that Job gained. God commissioned Job to intercede on behalf of his friends, who themselves had displayed a flawed understanding of God's ways. Also, the Bible says Job's captivity was turned (Job 42:10), and he received twice as much as he previously had. All the family members and friends that were absent during his struggle reappeared, and many of them gave him material blessings (Job 42:11).

God blessed Job with twice the amount of livestock he had at the beginning and gave him children as well: seven sons and three daughters. When his season of shame was over, he had more than ever! I'm sure that in the midst of it, the sudden loss looked permanent to Job and to those around him. They didn't see how he would ever recover.

But what they didn't know was that God never starts something without the end product in mind. He does not play with us as if we are chess pieces, basing His strategy on the moves of His opponent, trying to guess what the next move will be. God is omniscient; He knows everything! And before He allows you to walk into a season of shame, He already has the restoration plan worked out. I'm reminded of an old song that says that while we are trying to figure things out, God has already worked them out!

As Job is our witness, no matter how much we lose, if we maintain our integrity, restoration will come.

This lesson is a hard one to learn. We go through seasons of shame without a clue as to the outcome—we have no idea what God is doing. Our natural eyes may only see calamity, but our spiritual eyes must see eternity. That's what God sees. He knows the end from the beginning. We have to trust Him to release our due season at just the right time according to His plan.

Like Job, I have lost it all. But also like Job, my relationship with God grew and changed throughout my season of shame. Part of the restoration process was moving from a habit of church attendance and activity to having a consistent and real relationship with the Lord. By accepting

Christ as Lord and Savior sincerely and repenting of my misdeeds and misconceptions, I learned that God's plan for my life is greater than any ideas I had. Now I am able to do all things through Christ, knowing that He truly loves me. I can serve because I love Him, not out of a twisted sense of obligation. I can see His hand at work in my life in many ways, not the least of which is Him directing my steps to the role of pastor. That was a far different direction than what I planned for myself, but I see the Lord at work in our church and that blesses my soul.

The Lord restored me through time and opportunity. I am blessed to say that in my career I received promotions that moved me from a secretarial position (which I loved, by the way), to the paralegal profession. I have been afforded the opportunity to teach classes for the Department of Justice National Advocacy Center, teaching employees from all over the country. In addition, I have written legal briefs and documents for court, all without a formal legal education! The attorneys that I have worked with over the years tutored and trained me, and now I am a recognized professional. Not bad for a teenage mother who almost dropped out of high school. Only the Lord can deliver like that!

On the family side, Darryl and I are having a great time. We have a stable life and enjoy spending time together.

I get to see my grandkids nearly every weekend, and my daughter and I have a great relationship. I have learned to pray about things rather than stressing out and acting like everything that happens is about me. My heart is trusting, and I laugh more easily now. And even though I am not rich by any means, I have more than ever before! Every business venture hasn't been as successful as I'd hoped, but I have learned valuable lessons through every attempt I've made, and God has worked every experience to my advantage. Far from the fragile divorced woman I once was, there is a new confidence on the inside of me that is not based on material possessions. It is not diminished by what I have done or what I have been through. It is based on what Christ accomplished on the cross.

And I am writing! I know that I have truly survived my seasons of shame because I am now able to share with others the things that I have gone through. Instead of hiding my failures and living a counterfeit life, I choose to be open and honest about the things I have suffered. As I often say, at this point, I don't have anything to hide. There is no blackmail material here because I tell it all myself. After all, you don't know like I know what the Lord has done for me! If you read this book's introduction closely, you will see that it was difficult for me to write this book. It took me a lot longer than I thought it should have. Shame still had a grip on me in a few areas, but finishing this book has helped me to shake loose the last vestiges of shame in my life. I have survived my seasons of shame, even those that were self-inflicted, and so can you! And even though there may be more trials ahead of me, I know from experience that triumph is possible through Jesus Christ. I am writing, and I am free! It's starting to look like due season.

Survival Strategies

- ❖ Believe that God has a due season for you. Talk about it, pray for it, and expect it to come to pass. Cast a vision of what you want God's restoration to look like in your life. Be positive that God has a good plan for your life, but don't be afraid to pour your heart out to Him when things look bleak.
- ❖ Sow good seeds. It is both naturally and spiritually true that we reap what we sow, whether good or bad. If we are expecting restoration, harvest, and abundance, we must act like it. I am not advocating fakery; I encourage you to do your absolute best with what you have. Bless others when given the opportunity to do so. Become a giver and an intercessor.
- ❖ Release your expectations into God's hands. He is capable of handling them. Keep in mind, however, that He will not always give you what you want.

Often you receive what you need because God's perspective is greater than ours. He knows what will keep us in line with His plan for our lives and what will cause us to detour from His will.

6

Final Thoughts

> Finally, brothers, whatever is true, whatever is noble, whatever is right, whatever is pure, whatever is lovely, whatever is admirable—if anything is excellent or praiseworthy—think about such things. Whatever you have learned or received or heard from me, or seen in me—put it into practice. And the God of peace will be with you.
>
> —Philippians 4:8–9

BELIEVE IT OR not, I am writing the final chapter before I even finish writing this book. I can do that because no matter what else the book contains of my life, I want you to walk away from this book not thinking of me but thinking of yourself.

I am sure that you have had a variety of experiences, some of which may make what I have recorded here pale in comparison. I hope that is not the case, but I recognize that many people have been through far worse than I have. I also know that some people cannot even imagine the stuff that has happened to me.

Wherever you find yourself in the realm of experience, whether you have been publicly humiliated or have suffered in silence, seemingly unnoticed, there is something you need to know. You need to know that your life is not only determined by the things that you have been through. To a greater extent, your life depends on how you respond to the hard times of life. You are the beneficiary or victim of your responses.

It is nearly impossible to respond to tragedy, hardship, embarrassment, suffering, or adverse circumstances in a way that leads to a greater life without a personal relationship with God through Jesus Christ. If you happened to read through this entire book without being a Christian, won't you take a moment to pray for salvation? It doesn't take a long prayer or flowery prose. I am including some information at the end of this book that should help you on your journey toward Christ.

It is my personal testimony that in spite of the things that have happened to me, the Lord has kept my mind. When I wanted to lose it, He reminded me that I did not have to. When I wanted to kill myself, it was faith in God that kept me from doing that. Time and time again I have turned to the Word of God, the Bible, for comfort, for guidance, and for sanity. I want you to know the Bible has never failed me. In addition, prayer has been key; speaking to the Lord and allowing Him to speak to me through the Bible and through select people has made all the difference in my life.

You may not know where to look for help to get through your season of shame. I want to suggest that you start with Romans 8. It makes it clear that you do not have to hold on to guilt or shame if you are in Christ Jesus. From the outset, the message of the chapter is that you are not under condemnation; God does not hold your wrong against you, and He does not condemn you for the things that you have been through. You should take some time to read the entire chapter and ask the Holy Spirit to show you just who you are in the context of the Scripture.

Romans 8:28 gives us this precious message to hold on to throughout our season of shame: "And we know that in all things God works for the good of those who love him, who have been called according to his purpose."

I read this passage over and over again before I really understood its message. The Scripture does not promise us that everything that happens in our lives will be good. Rather, it lets us know that no matter what is happening,

God is working behind the scenes to work things out for our ultimate good.

Once you get a grasp on this truth, it makes a powerful difference in your life. So many times, especially as Christians, we have a glorified view of the world—one in which we believe we are exempt from suffering because we belong to the Lord. If you read the Scripture and particularly the examples that have been given in this book, you will see that is far from the truth. God allows His people to suffer, but He makes some promises that help you make it through.

Here is another powerful promise from the Bible that is one to turn to when you are in the midst of a season of shame:

> You will keep in perfect peace him whose mind is steadfast, because he trusts in you. Trust in the LORD forever, for the LORD, the LORD, is the Rock eternal. (Isa. 26:3–4)

You can depend on the Lord to keep (meaning "guard" or "protect") your mind if you put your trust in Him. The Lord is unchanging; He remains the same according to Hebrews 13:8: "Jesus Christ is the same yesterday and today and forever." His power and ability has not diminished at all from the earliest of times. He can and will deliver you, but it may not always be at the time or in the way that you desire. You have to trust Him.

Trusting God is a big part of surviving your season of shame. You have seen it work throughout this book. But there is something else that we must do that is just as difficult: trust yourself.

Forgive yourself for your past failures, mistakes, and sins, and be determined to start over again with a new mind-set. It is important that you develop a godly character to the point where you can trust yourself to respond appropriately in the midst of trouble. One of the key ways to make this happen is to actively work to renew your mind. Here is the biblical evidence that this is necessary:

> Therefore, I urge you, brothers, in view of God's mercy, to offer your bodies as living sacrifices, holy and pleasing to God—this is your spiritual act of worship. Do not conform any longer to the pattern of this world, but be transformed by the renewing of your mind. Then you will be able to test and approve what God's will is—his good, pleasing and perfect will. For by the grace given me I say to every one of you: Do not think of yourself more highly than you ought, but rather think of yourself with sober judgment, in accordance with the measure of faith God has given you. (Rom. 12:1–3)

Until you renew your mind, you can only respond to trouble the way the world responds—with retaliation, unforgiveness, hatred, bitterness, and self-pity. You are destined to suffer in ways that do not work for your good if you respond according to earthly, sensual wisdom. You have to immerse yourself in the Word of God in order to be able to tap into God's wisdom in every situation you face.

God's wisdom does not come to us naturally; we must ask for it. The Bible lets us know that we have to ask in faith; that's the trusting God that I spoke about earlier.

> If any of you lacks wisdom, he should ask God, who gives generously to all without finding fault, and it will be given to him. But when he asks, he must believe and not doubt, because he who doubts is like a wave of the sea, blown and tossed by the wind. That man should not think he will receive anything from the Lord; he is a double-minded man, unstable in all he does. (James 1:5–8)

God will keep you stable in the midst of your suffering, and when your suffering in an area of your life is complete, He will do even more for you.

> And the God of all grace, who called you to his eternal glory in Christ, after you have suffered a

little while, will himself restore you and make you strong, firm and steadfast. (1 Pet. 5:10)

By the way, the book of 1 Peter gives a great perspective on suffering. It is written by a man that had been through so much, first as a hotheaded disciple of the Lord Jesus Christ, then as a leader of the early church. He learned firsthand what suffering could accomplish in the life of a believer and wrote his letters to encourage others that would walk the path he knew so well. I encourage you to read his writings to help you in your own walk through the dark days of life.

In addition, there is a passage of Scripture at the beginning of this chapter that is crucial to your survival—I affectionately call it "The List." It is important because it serves as a checklist of ways to filter your thoughts so that you do not dwell on the negative things that happen to you. I find—and I hope you will also—that as you measure your thoughts against this list, you will begin to concentrate more on what God is doing through your life than what the enemy is doing to your life. The list will help you to think in a healthy, positive way. Take a look at it one more time:

> Finally, brothers, whatever is true, whatever is noble, whatever is right, whatever is pure, whatever is lovely, whatever is admirable—if anything is excellent or praiseworthy—think about such things. Whatever

you have learned or received or heard from me, or seen in me—put it into practice. And the God of peace will be with you. (Phil. 4:8–9)

In this book you have read about me—not everything I could have told, but just what is necessary to the task. But more importantly, you have read about people who have walked through the fiery trials of life and come out with victory! In every instance, including mine, God worked it out for His glory. Believe it or not, that is our highest calling: to bring glory to God through our lives.

I have prayed, cried, and labored over this book so that we can all be delivered. It took a long time to finish it because it is very personal to me. It is my sincerest hope that something you read has struck a chord or struck a nerve in areas where you need to trust God. I hope that you have laughed and cried along with me in this journey.

I also hope that you have seen some of the characters in this book in new and exciting ways. I hope you are motivated to endure and that you see that no matter what, with God and through Christ, you can survive.

These are my parting thoughts.

Are You Saved?

Salvation is not about being part of a particular religion or denomination. It is about the finished work of Jesus Christ, who died on the cross for our sins and rose again so that we might have eternal life. If you have not accepted Jesus as your Lord and Savior, you are not saved. But the great thing about salvation is that you don't have to be in a church to get saved. You can give your life to Jesus right now. It's this simple:

1. Recognize that God loves you and desires that you be saved.

   > For God loved the world in this way: He gave His One and Only Son, so that everyone who believes in Him will not perish but have eternal life. For God did not send His Son into the world that He might condemn the world, but that the world might be saved through Him. (John 3:16–17)

2. Acknowledge that you are a sinner that needs to be saved. We all start out that way, so you are not alone. There is no need for shame or fear.

For all have sinned and fall short of the glory of God. (Rom. 3:23)

3. Recognize that sin has a penalty, but Christ has paid it.

    For the wages of sin is death, but the gift of God is eternal life in Christ Jesus our Lord. (Rom. 6:23)

4. Accept Jesus Christ as Lord and Savior. The gift is free, but we don't actually possess it until we reach out to receive it.

    If you confess with your mouth, "Jesus is Lord," and believe in your heart that God raised Him from the dead, you will be saved. With the heart one believes, resulting in righteousness, and with the mouth one confesses, resulting in salvation. (Rom. 10:9–10)

5. Ask God to forgive your sins.

    If we confess our sins, He is faithful and righteous to forgive us our sins and to cleanse us from all unrighteousness. (1 John 1:9)

Now that you have information, take action! Pray a simple prayer like this one:

> Lord, I realize that I am a sinner, and I need to be saved. I confess that I have sinned, and I ask You to forgive me and make me clean. Right now, I ask Jesus to come into my life and be my Lord and Savior. Thank You for accepting and saving me. Thank You for giving me eternal life. In Jesus's name I pray. Amen.

Now you are saved! One of the best things to do in order for your salvation to feel real is to tell somebody. If you don't know anyone that you can tell, get in contact with me by e-mail at pastorcmblount@gmail.com. Heaven is rejoicing, and so are we!

It is also very important that you make a break with sin. You should turn away from everything you know is displeasing to God. You may not even know what displeases God, but if it is hurtful to yourself or to others, you should do your best to let it go.

You should also find a church where you can grow in your newfound faith. Just make sure that the church believes that Jesus Christ is Lord and the Son of God and that their teachings are based on the Holy Bible. Our church, Eternal Word Fellowship, welcomes you to contact us for help at eternalwordfellowship@gmail.com.

Welcome to the family of God

www.ingramcontent.com/pod-product-compliance
Lightning Source LLC
Chambersburg PA
CBHW072058290426
44110CB00014B/1734